Let Us Again

Writings and Paintings by

Tom Gick

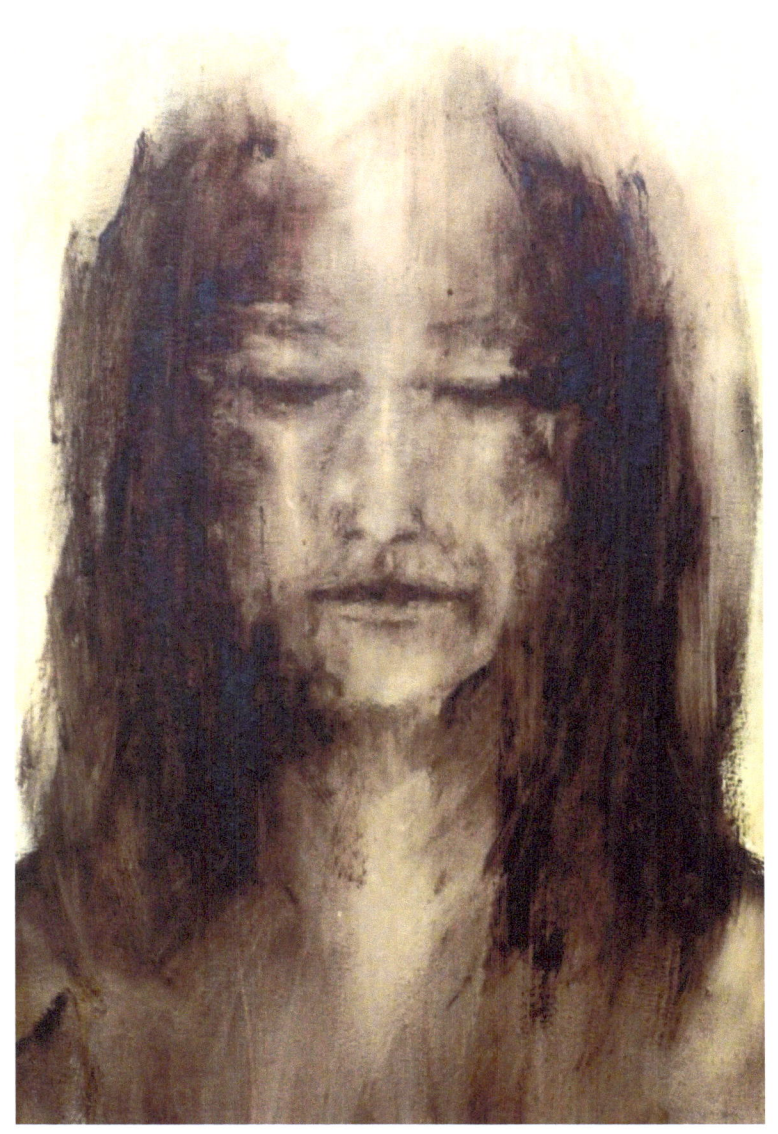

Let Us Again

A road stretches into the far distance, covered with snow, unbroken and without footprints. I look to where it ends. I have been going such a long way and am tired. I look back into the past and see that there are no footprints, and for the first time I realize that the journey and the arrival are the same. I go on, my steps breaking into the silent snow, quietly and surely going on. I know that if I open my eyes the road and its efforts will disappear. When I open my eyes, the long time it took to go on will be forgotten. Where do I begin, the ending of my life embraced in my long beginning, my eternity giving time back to itself. I know that this beginning reaches both into the past and the future simultaneously, forever both what has happened and what will happen. I spend my time pretending that I know the separateness of time. I am waiting and remembering and forgetting. So very long. And I have been going on for so long that I at last know that I am no longer the dreamer, but have become the dream. You recognize the difference through lifetimes of being. I close my eyes tonight and will be remembered by it all, by the synchronicity of matter and mind in miracle. I am old in my waiting.

***

Through Union, to Thomaston, to Rockland, to Camden, To Belfast, to Unity, to Liberty. It is the journey round place and time, from there to here, to you, the gathering of all from everywhere, the journey of heart and spirit and matter to each other, and then away, and which are united and which I almost lose, never have, and yet regain. It is the journey before and after. It is the call of all to all. It is the call of what happens now. No way to begin or to end, almost no way ever to be. Walk to the edge, the edge of the world, and stand on its spinning surface, the counter-clockwise whirling will titter you away and toward the ever-expanding creation. Slowly its exhaustion will still you and begin to spin clockwise tumbling you back into the center, into the arms of yourself. Fall out of the broken world, then eat, regain strength, and fall again. It is the walking from center to edge and back again, from edge to center and back again. And the hand that spins you is your own and all the separate and unified parts of what the spinning creates. The hand and the host come first and are there last. Or the flight and the spinning come first and create the hand and host. Or they are the same. Or they are separate. Or it is the heartbeat thus created. Or it is the loving created by this heartbeat. It is the wanting to go home. Through Union to Hope to Liberty. Or it is the home wanting to come. Or it is the wild waste. Or it is the emptiness and the fullness. It is the hunger. It is the banquet. It is the eating and the full belly. It is the sickness and the release of hunger. It is the need to eat again. It is the coursing of sustenance through the body. The foot bone's connected to the ankle bone, the ankle bone's connected to the leg bone, the leg bone's connected to the knee bone... And that's the way of the Lord. It is the home. It is the going home. It is the leaving. It is the far field where the home is. It is the building of a home. It is the journey from field to home to field and back again. It is the flight of birds from nest to nourishment to nest. It is the nest. It is the nourishment. It is the field over which they fly. It is the green of the field, the blue of the sky, the yellow of the sun that lights the field, it is the red of their feathers, their passion to fly. It is the light beyond them all. It is all. It is nothing. It is the light of day that gathers the night back into the day. It is the moon that gathers light into the night. It is the gathering. It can't go on. It goes on. It is it in whatever strength and startle and beauty battling to reach home. It is rest when found, when beauty, freedom, love, is known and accepted. It is the other, the self, the two, the one. It is separate. It is joined. It is. It is not. And it is to be, to become, to be becoming, to be becoming being. It is to find thee, to find me. It is a castle, a kingdom come, a home, a child. It is me, it is not me, it is everybody, it is nobody. It is a richness, a poverty. It can't go on, it goes on, forever. It is a pure and impure state of intuition. It is everything relating to everything. It is nothing relating to nothing. It is everything relating to nothing. I need to put away, to pull shut the curtain, to go to sleep. Then I will search for first things first, for foundations, for Maineland, for a home. Help me find rest, if only the rest of one night.

It is all that I can do. I cannot go on with the purity of intuition purifying itself.

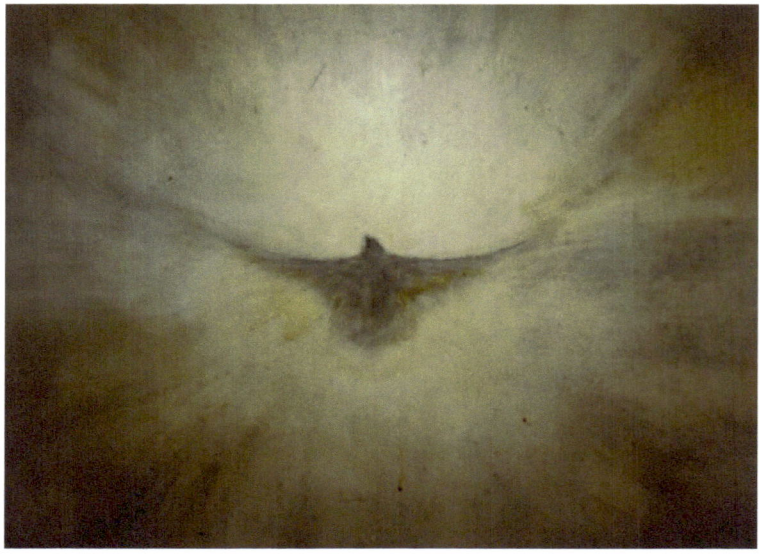

***

I am in an enormous room. Did I dream of it or did it dream me here? I once believed that things were separate, that words were a sign, a way of naming what is, that thought and dream, action, place, were things that you had, that happened to you, that there was a space between it all, room to breathe. There is no room. Everything every moment is both attention and intention at the same time, the communion of place and time and self into the experience of their uniting beyond not only mind but even perception and presence. It is the journey through ravishment home to the body we share with everything. It is an enormous room. My long, my lost, I cannot even breathe. What am I to do? What is the structure of myself? My body cannot endure. Is there any longer a belief in the miraculous, in a madness that is divine, in a transformative vision at the very center of matter that creates all that is? All I know is that tonight there is no place to go. I cannot leave this room because there is no place neither here nor elsewhere. In the space of infinite loss there is no time. Time and space become what they truly are, parts of our self. What seems away flows back into the self. My life seeps like old blood flowing from me in images of my dream. It is painful to stay and yet impossible to leave. It is how I lose what I am to find again what I am. I will wrap myself in a quilt of many colors and sleep into this dream. Tomorrow I will go on.

I am awake and it is early and it goes on. It is a wake. It truly is awake, the wisdom of life to know freely when to sleep, when to wake, a rhythm of walking, waiting, sleeping, awakening. The journal continues, the journey forever. I can go on. I am a wondrous child in the center of a wondrous embrace, beyond the tears, yet reaching to a heart and tears I know are there forever. I go, I come, I sleep, I awaken, I love, I go again. I am the going back that goes on. I change, I stay I become what I am, say what I am. Tomorrow is Sunday, tomorrow is time for me to leave and go home. Tomorrow is a way to go home. The wind gathers me in its roaring, quiet flow and I become the wind cascading nowhere and everywhere. It is now raining outside, washing me back into the earth. I begin again to eat, be eaten, to sleep, to be. I begin again, begin again.

***

Ah my death, what life you give me. All boundaries are collapsing, the heart, the mind, time, space, my very body. The world, a room, a snow-covered path, the flesh, the mind, are spirit, and spirit is matter. They are no longer separate and one a reflection of the other. They are identical. Relating, when surrendered to fully, becomes identity. Everything I do, I am, where I live, the objects I dream and make, all the things before my eyes are completely and profoundly transcendent and immanent at the same time. I and the world are one in miracle. The lawn where I walk is my skin, the room where I love and betray is my body, the furnace I feed to warm my home is my heart consuming it all. And I know the sheer correspondence of words, place, self, in the transmutation of the body of the world, the marriage wherein identity and separateness embrace in union, a long life that stretches, like embraced arms, time and space, who and what and where I am across the eternity of my shape.

***

It is what we know and do not know. It is what we are and are not. It is a feast and a starvation. It is the primary colors of our world and it is the white of light. It is a quiet and it is a scream. It is the stillness and the whirlwind. It is the space between

and it is the now of their union. Sum, eram, ero, fui,
fueram, fuero, sim, essem, fueram, fuissam, es, esse. I
am, I was, I shall be, I have been, I had been, I shall
have been, may I be, I should be, I may have been, I
shall have been, may I be, I should be, I may have
been, I should have been, be thou, be. And meanings
of the tenses are so varied and so many that no
attempt can be made to give them. And the attempt to
give them can be made. Amo, amas, amat, amamus,
amatis, amant. And it goes on again. And then back
again. And again. Intuit, into it again. I intuit the
world, the world intuits me. We dance, resonate, we
fall into pieces. We fall together again and again and
forever again. It is what is, the passages of now
separating and joining, the act and action and finally
presence of again. And such a wondrous, terrifying
playing of hide and seek, hide and find. Come out
and play. Would you meet me, have you met me, may
you meet me, meet me. You know what they're
talking about. It's a game called love and be. And if
you see her, say hello, tell her it ain't why. It just is
again and again. Be the return. Be being and be
separateness. And now I whirl and spin and stop and
rest and love and think and feel and again and again.
You must become what you dream, through the varied
passages of day and night. The key is to dream well,
to dream what is needed, to dream steadfastly and
beyond doubt to love and be loved. The far field is
beyond Unity, past Hope, past Liberty, to where all
places contain themselves. It is the love, birth, death,
rebirth, time, space, emptiness, fullness, ecstasy,
despair, sadness, joy, all the healing rolling rhythm of
its green grass, the whirlwind and the quiet, the

tranquility, and magic of again without anything to do but to be. It is the far field of pure and impure intention, of subjective and objective transcendence, the reconciliation beyond the garden. It is a long way to go.

***

My home is full of gold. Yellow birds are everywhere. Gold is splashed on all the walls surrounding me. The world I dream and live is in flames. The light is stripping me to my very bones. I only know that this communion is a bodily moment where matter and spirit meet. The basis of what is real is in this meeting. My life as separate is ended and now belongs to the heart of the world. I have finally, after all these years of wandering, fallen into the flowing robe of life. I am one. "Ah my dear, fall, gall thyself, and gash gold-vermillion."

***

I do not know what I do. I do not know who I am. I am so solid in myself and so completely empty. Time and space, here or there, you and me, always or never, stay or go. I thought that Liberty was a place, that where I loved, that whom I loved was another. Today I know it is all a state of mind and a state of matter, a sacred intention constantly interpenetrating a state of nature. There are no separations in your ravishing dark eyes. We live our lives sure we know what is. We know what it is to know, to see and touch, to have a body and a world, to grow and to die and to love between the two. We know and yet we do not know. Everything we do, all we are and have is immanent and yet at the same moment transcendent. The ecstasies of our experience are a prelude to the fuller ecstasy of our union with all that is. By our birthing we leave a world of boundaries and begin a journey through another's body into the wonder of light. The next time we make the journey in our own bodies. The last time we make the same voyage in God's body. And then we look back as children and realize all these bodies are the same. All structures are without boundaries in that they contain and describe and become all other structures. We are as solid as the trees outside our windows and at the same time as utterly seen. We are the shape of the world and the content of experience, a shape that can be seen, felt, known, given away, by looking closely at all that is with the wisdom and love to realize that you are looking at yourself. All is pure intention, the constantly repeated shape of relatedness and identity beyond anything imagined. I stand surrounded by gold-vermillion, in the embrace of a love that is transparent, arisen from the ashes of how I once loved. I have fallen through death into an unconditional and eternal love. It is impossible to stand as before, with a body seemingly as before and yet to feel you have passed through. Everything is forever changed, the limit of love, the boundness of the body, the forsaken knowing of the mind.

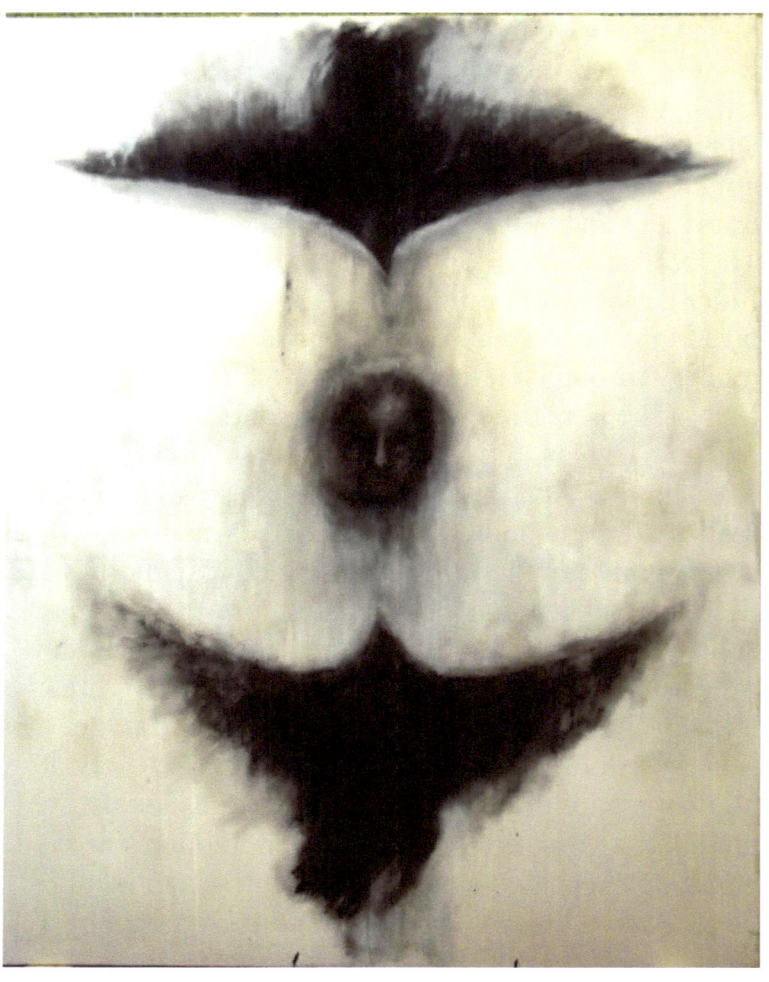

***

Days and nights of sleeplessness filled with a shaking and total disintegration, a journey into a ravaged heart, a gathering of all I have experienced and thought and dreamt exploding into all dreams. I am roaring the fire of a dragon burning everything, thought and intention, emotion and body. The dazzle of mind and memory, dreams and reality consumed. My spirit is dying, and in its greatest agony I cannot help. The doors of perception are wide open and the door is the gaping mouth of a dragon.

***

Dear Spirit, come back from your flights away from the field, come back from your flights to the far field, your mad, frenzied voyages in terror and startle. You soar away frightened and return momentarily transformed and enhanced, only to become startled again and fly madly to yet another place where you think you are safe. The only real safety, to return to where I am, and together we will begin again our search for your frightened love. She too is frightened and soaring wildly away. We can heal and restore ourselves if only we search for her. It may take a while but we can find and know her.

***

I start all over again, to walk, eat, reason, love, to die. How free I am. I go on, up the sloping field that borders the house. Still, surrounded by trees, empty, I fall beyond it all, beyond the deaths and births into a unity that gathers all states, all mind, all my body. A feast of all reality, all opposites, all mansions, the constant embracing flow of everything to all things. To ask of life why is finally without meaning. I stand flowing into everything yet flowing into nothing because a part of everything. There is no place to go in this fullness, no effort, no loss, no cost, a self-contained perfection of motion and stillness, being and becoming, separateness and duality and union, the many that is one, the one that is many. It is everything and all. It is unconditional relationality, neither subject nor object, but both. I and thou at one. And I stand a flowing stillness, a center that is a surround and a surround without a center, a flower unfolding and infolding, a pulsating without end. It is fullness without source, without beginning or end, an eternity of love expressing all creation, an embracing with arms open wide. I cling to nothing yet hold all things in an enclosure that offers freedom. My breath swirls back into my face breathing together all that I gather.

***

The door to the house is closed and I have left. My face is burnt black, my body in ashes, my mind in constant communion. My days pass as I dissolve and spill into all that is. There is nothing but everything, every second.

***

12

It is the far field, it is the garden, it is the far field near, it is the passage, the walking from one to the other. It is a garden to be planted, a field to be harvested. It is the planting, it is the reaping. It is the blood coursing, circulating through the body. It is the body, it is the blood. It is love travelling from the body to the heart to the mind to the soul to God to itself. And it is love's falling back through, back to the body. It is the falling, it is the vessel filling and emptying. Got to go back. Got to go back. And I don't know why, I just got to go back. Sleep like a baby again, wake every few hours, ask for nourishment. Awake, asleep. From the womb to the womb and back again. After the agony and wonder of birth I am living the cycle of a newborn. I am resurrected again. I am my grandmother standing strong and with love waiting for her lover. And you finally arrive, you are now, a moment cascading and flowing in and out, again and again now. And you return to what, to who, to where you were, only possessing the gift of now, of pure being aware of itself being aware. And your only life's work is to stay aware, stay alert to what you always had and always did. It is the wisdom of love and the love of wisdom. It is a way to know and how to not know. It is the knowledge of all and the emptiness of all knowledge. It is the mind stretched beyond all bearing where only feeling remains. It is feeling trying to remember its source. It is feeling trying to think again without thinking. It is the forgetting and the trying not to forget. It is the forgetting, it is the remembering. It is the time it takes to forget, to remember. It is the memory of time. It is the time of forgetting the memory. It is once again. It is again once. It is time to build a bird feeder, to watch in relation the birds coming and going from nest to flight to feed. It is time to till a garden in the far field, to plant flowers, to allow birds to drop their seeds that will mix and grow with the flowers. It is time to watch and be the ceremony of hunger, flight, a place to go and a place to be. It is time to be again. It is the mind beyond imaging. It is the dream you dream, the dream you change, the change you dream. It is the mind beyond dreaming, dreaming beyond itself. And it is my grandmother's long dreaming of me. And it is my dreaming of my grandmother. It is the standing still after the long walking. It is the journey from there to here to now. It is her image again, against the white wall. It is the wall. It is the space to be. It is me and it is her, and it is the wall we fall against. And it is finally together again, all the pieces, all the horses, all the king's men. I can't go on. I go on again. I gather all the pieces. There are no pieces. I gather, I scatter. I am the king who scatters, who gathers, who sows, who reaps, who thinks, who loves, who has, who has not, who remembers, who forgets, who dreams, who wakes, who is, who is not, who goes on, who stays, who dreams and wakes again. Past Thomaston, through Hope, to Liberty, to Maineland again. Would you meet me, would you meet me in the country? It's not why, it just is. It' a long way, a long way coming, it's a long way to go. It is the foot I kiss, the ankle I massage, the leg I stroke, the breast I fall onto, the neck I caress, the eyes I kiss, the mind I touch and love again. And it is the sun in the morning slanting through the window. It is the

*reflection that is in the window. It is the round face
that answers the round sun. It is going round and
round. It is going around. It is a long, long way
around. It is the heart in the body, the sun in the face.
It is the body in the heart, the face in the sun. It is
every morning again. It is again. It is the mind
carnate, re-incarnate. It is the womb. It is the fetus.
It is the joined source of them both. It is the heart in
the mind, the mind in the heart. It is the shape of a
face. It is the shape of a heart. It is the shape of
relating. It is the search for the mother. It is the
search for the father. It is the union that gives birth.
It is a child's search for parents. It is the parent's
search for children. It is always, forever. It is again.
And you have to leave again in order to come back
again. And you have to come back again in order to
leave, again and again. It is the search for creation.
It is the journey to creation. It is the desire for
creation. It is creation, recreated again and again.
The collapse into the unconscious is the fall into the
conscious again. It is the call of the unknown
answered by the known. It is the cry of the heart
healed by the body. It is the mind and the heart and
the body united again. It is the careening and the
cascading of all to all and always again. It is forever
physical presence. It is the hand, the eye, the words,
the mind, the coherence, the reverie of everything. It
is the brush and the canvas and the surface of color.
It is the awe and awful presence of matter, the body
and skin and blood of transcendence. And it is again
and again, in sleep again and in the sun again. And
it doesn't matter what is said. And it doesn't matter
what is done. All that matters is my relationship, all*

that matters is my relating. And again I will take you in my arms. And again we will go round in a circle, around and around again. And it is to fall further, and it is to fall farther, and it is to turn in a circle round and round. And it is to die, and it is to live in a circle round and around again. It is to be again. And it is not hope nor despair, not answer nor call, not acceptance nor will, not thought nor dream, not near nor far, not self nor other, not home nor away nor body nor soul nor loss nor gain. Only again.

***

And Dear Spirit, it is now only a matter of time. Only now. We must wait for the rain. Then we can begin our search for content. And we will find it where we left it, where we lost it, there from the beginning. Now only. Never truly lost, never forgotten. That is how we will find it. That is why we will find it. Through all the tenses and conjugations, through all the thoughts and words, through Union, past Thomaston, past Hope, to Liberty. What is forgotten is remembered, what is hidden is found, what is left is returned. What becomes, is. What we dream, where we go, is one day really now. Let the rain fall and fill the far field, splash our faces and cascade down our eyes and return us back. And we will kiss the tears from our eyes. Let the trees stand but a few feet apart, far and near, their limbs arching, where red and yellow and blue birds mix and nest. And we are all only in the rain, and in the sun, in the night, and in the day.

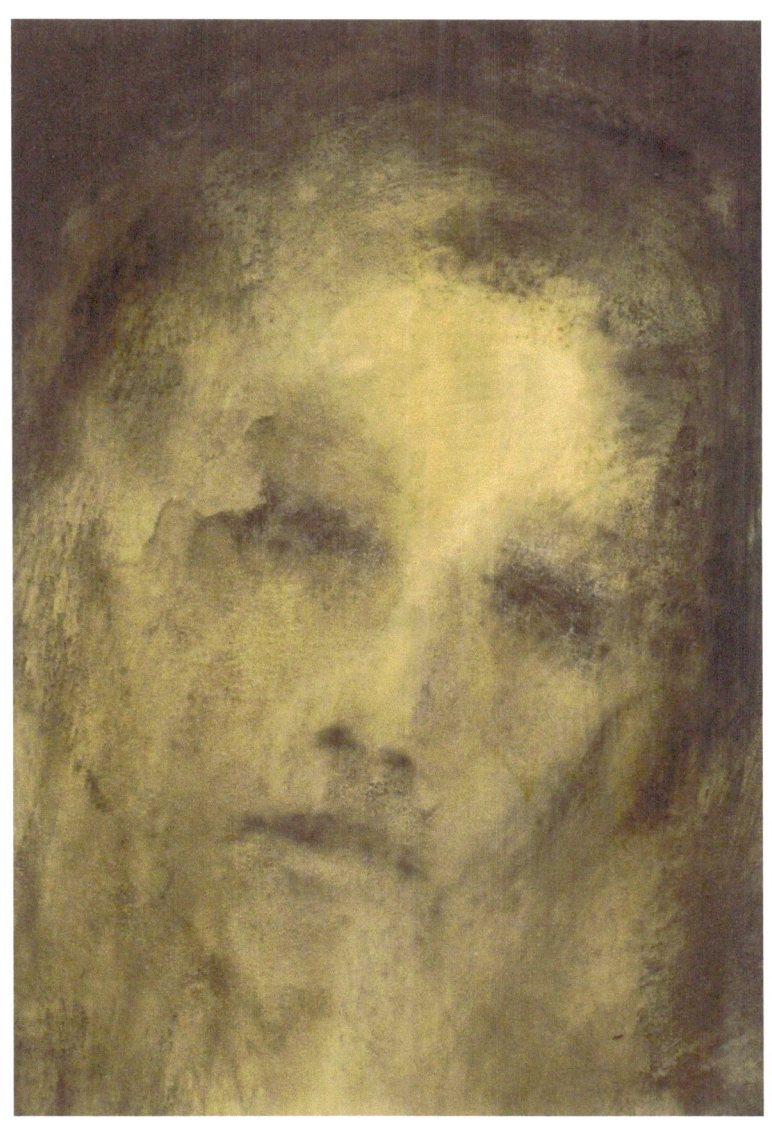

***

    I know all is a dream, but a different manner of dream, where the contents are real. I watch myself in all others, all thoughts and actions, all objects. I am identical to all my awareness and body touches. And neither my awareness nor myself is any longer mine. To think and to feel are finally identical. To live and to die are impossible. A child's voice recites in piercing staccato the alphabet, the archaic sound of the mind in its earliest love. To be born again, to begin all over again, to start at the beginning, a child of creation, beyond fear, beyond pain, to the bliss of openness and exploration, a sun making reality, a golden flame vibrating in the wind and sending itself in all directions. Recalling, the mind and heart explode into vastness, into an integrity of ever greater moments of unity. I die a thousand deaths daily, my body falling from me like dying leaves. Many a tear has to fall. All fall down. I collapse daily clinging to my breath, to what is left of myself and to all of myself that is passing away. And yet it is impossible to cling. A childlike world of identity of subject and object, of pure synchronicity, a world of unending attention, an awareness that is the gathering of the embrace of an all-pervading love. All my life, all my dreams, all my failures, is being gathered and thrown into an all-consuming fire. Nothing is left as it once was. The sheer reality of my body, my sight, my acts, my mind, are charred into the ashes of this crucifixion. I am being set free of the pain of who I am. I am journeying into God's pain, into the giving of everything.

I can't go on again. I am too tired, beyond the words, the mind, the pain of separateness and unity. And I go on. I do not go on. I will not go on. I should not go on. The path past Unity to Hope to Liberty is too long a way to go. Please let me go, let me stop. I am, I was, I shall be. Let me be. Let the whirl of my white sleeves gather all and be gathered to all again and again and again. Let the morning be over for a while. Let me walk quietly to the center of the far field to wait for our return, to watch in peace and communion the birds soaring above our heads, to slowly arch our arms to the sun, the wind, the rain. It is at last all we can do, wait in wonder and hope and surprise for the sun in our eyes again. And the waiting is the strength we search for all our lives and possess all our lives. It is the manner of the child who dismembers her play and waits for something to put it back together. It is what allows for dismemberment, for recreation and creation. It is the wisdom of the field that gathers us all, awaits us, releases us, and rejoins us. It is beyond to let me be, beyond the cry to be left and the terror to be. It is beyond being to being in love. It is the agony and final choice of time and space, of creation and created. It is the journey of being to become, to give its solitude away, again and again and forever. It is the birth of being and becoming and their union beyond each other. It is past Unity, past Hope, to Liberty. It is the freeing on time to eternity, to a gathering of itself to itself, to a gathering of all place.

***

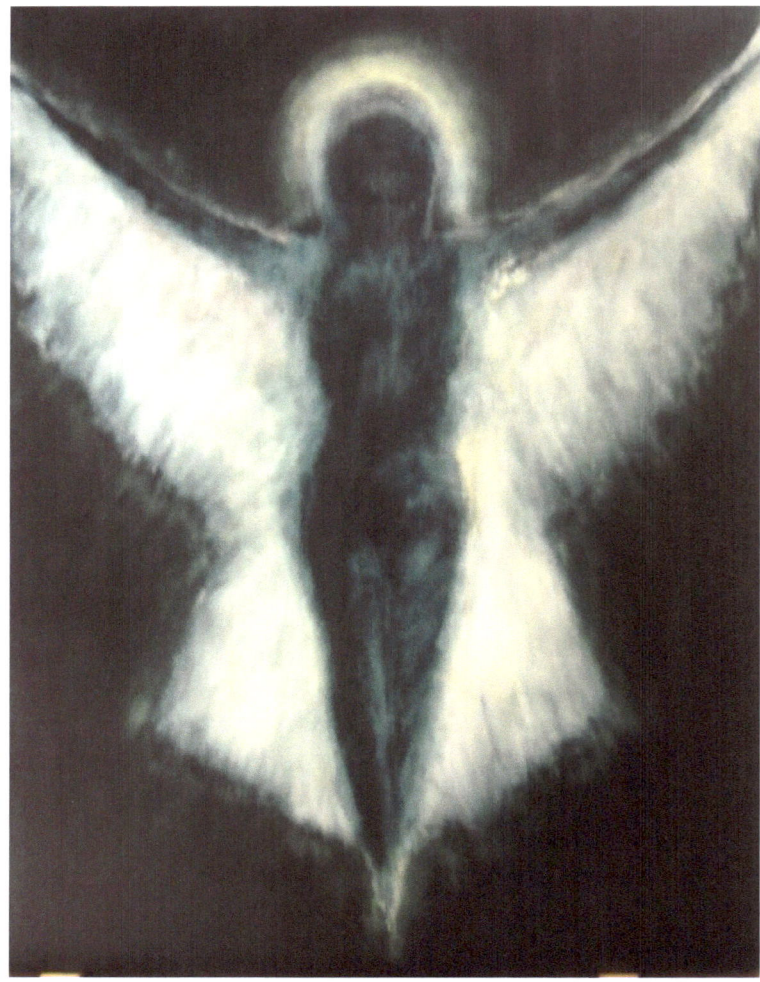

I'm drunk these days, intoxicated by all I am. I am in the heart of the country surrounded by spacious fields. I have lived an unending separateness and I have lived an unending unity. I spend each day at the end of dying, counting my breaths, trying to allow the freedom at the end of the mind. I almost rarely ask why. I have so far to go and I know once I arrive the arrival will be why. A heart unconditionally alert, vastly sensate, is a heart that has died a thousand deaths and finds it impossible to die. Look if you must into all the rooms of all the mansions. A dragon stands before each door and only if you become the dragon will you go inside. And the dragon and the door and the room and the home and you are the same. Enter your heart. Be unseparate in your ashes. I do not know what is there in the ashes, and yet if you were to look closely into my eyes I would have to tell you. I would, if you loved enough, want to tell you. Come into the flames of the heart and meet me as sacrifice. But be willing for your love to be enough to reach the imperishable.

Am I only at the beginning or am I also at the end? It is one thing to journey to the self, to watch in dreams, desires, thoughts, acts, surrender, the alchemy of transformation. But the transmutation of and into the self is only a prelude. The flower of the self once found then blows into the field of all creation.

**

Deep snow covers my life. I have withdrawn and am covered by the ancient quilt of my grandmother. My eyes are closed to the world as I sleep into my awakening. A hoarse, antique voice whispers--"If not you, nobody". A constant dialogue and call of pronouns, thee and me, I and thou. We are coming together in our long unity. I am breathing my own breath, drinking my own blood, saying my own voice.

***

Early morning and the prairie wind gathers across the fields. My few distractions will soon be swept away, gathered from field to field across the body of the country. I return to the interior, to the garden bordering this field, to say the praise and wonder of it, to mix the bright yellow of my heart with the deep green of this vast body.

***

My heart falls in the rain. The field and I are one. We are a skin of fallen leaves and old grass. Let my surrender be as this season. Let my arms arch the horizon and my face shape the trees and let the sun shine against us.

***

Dear Spirit, know that your flying is your rest, know that your exhaustion and waste is your capture and freedom. Let go and become arrival. The far field will gather you in its lush green heart and let you close your eyes to the night and to the day, to the wind and the rain. And I will rejoin you there and kiss your eyes and again awaken your heart. And we will know it is not the flight nor the arrival, not the wind nor the rain nor the sun, not the day nor the night, but all that matters is our relationship, all that matters is the field that contains us and frees us. And field will call to field. And far will call to near. And the far field will answer the near field. And where all is scattered in many places all will be gathered together again. And dream and matter will answer each other again. And we will no longer go past Unity to Hope to Liberty, but will gather place and time, going and coming, dreamer and dream, and be free again to be the far field near again. And we will embrace each other and know that to become lovers is to be, and know that our long becoming is our final being, our being in love in the field.

***

I close my mind and see a child with dark radiant eyes wrapped in a shimmering white sheet. I am my child, my parent, my birth, my death. Beyond knowledge and clarity to vision, to presence, to the living of sight, where a dream is a thought, a thought is an object, where a noun is a verb, where God is everywhere and I live my children.

***

Tonight my legs ache and my body dissembles. My dream of myself is so close. In a few days I will move again to myself, to a place of sanctuary in the midst of an abundant life, a place where what is essential is what I will find, and what is left will find me, life's lullaby and my listening heart, a dream of love fulfilled in a field filled with golden flowers,

where the pulse of my heart throbs into the trees
surrounding.

***

Would you meet me in the country? The lawn
flashes with my million eyes tonight. Where are you?
I am here in the midst of myself and lost into another.
Our room we share is enormous as the infinite sharing
of our hearts. We stand but a few feet apart, our
branches touching, our bodies the world we shade,
dappled by wind and sun, flowing in stillness back
into ourselves, into our translucent surround of who
we are and what we live.

***

*Then nest will call to nest and bird will sing to
bird and both will fly to and dance the field. And
place will name place and time will recall time. And
the rainbow will gather color and green will be red
and blue will be yellow, and all will shine unmixed.
And the wind and the rain and the sun and the moon
and the day and the night will join, and the
generations and the passages will rest. And door and
the window will open and close as easily as the eye.
Then genesis and resurrection will join their work,
and living and imaging will embrace. Then to go on
and not to go on will be only a matter of time, the
closing of an eye, the opening of a heart, the standing
still in the field again. Let it come, come to it forever
and again. Become the breath that is the green of the
grass, the yellow of the birds, the shape of the leaves.*

Become the heartbeat of all and gather all and be gathered by all. And know for the first time and for the last time again and never again. It is the single sigh. It is the noun and the verb and it is unseparate, without past, present, future, without tense. It is it and it is, forever and again, always and never. It is without subject or object, only again and never again. It is the embrace of all. It is the letting go of all. It is the love of life and it is the life of love. It is Unity, it is Hope, it is Liberty. And it is the rest and stillness of again and again, of never and forever. It is both it and is again and never. It is both each again. It is both all again. It is yet and always again. It is our name again. It is a long way. It is to stay a long time. It is.

***

The walls of my interior are painted green and in the right light the trees outside my eyes approach so near. To be the moment before and after sight, identical to fullness and emptiness, the still roar of in and out, of sameness and reunion. I want always to live together in total correspondence of the self-emptying of the world and the self-emptying of myself, to live where love is pierced through and silently pours out its heart into the world, a life of pure relatedness of inside and outside. To divine reality as if by touching it without seeing it, in freedom and spaciousness, where I am without reflected meaning, where conscious occurrence and occurring consciousness meet, an unspeakable

25

fullness where wonder is regained and green is no longer merely paint.

***

I walk out of my sleep into a field, circling the silence of a structure that is myself. A light illuminates softly the interior. It is a structure with many rooms, and I have entered them all. A tree overhangs me, shaped like a cross, spreading its branches and reaching into a nearby field, dividing my upper from my lower, my right from my left. And hanging from the intersection of its main branches is a golden flower.

***

The marriage of thought and sensation, the making of a conscious body, and a vastness accepting fullness. Flow my tears, my rivers bath me, washing me into the ocean of mind and heart and body. I leave so much behind and I gather so much forgetfulness. My arms stretch the trees, my mind circles the heart, forming a center less circle, a swirl of water and leaves, a freedom beyond freedom, a circle beyond form, a motion beyond motion, a heart beyond itself. Beyond my desire to love and be loved, beyond my rhythms of life and death is my home, the body of creation, the eternity of intention. Beyond my life is the field of life, its trees stretching time, its leaves falling into space, its soil accepting it all. And letting it all is the heart of the field, the feel of the heart, the heart throbbing into forever to gather all to

unity and freedom. Let me be like falling leaves in
this season of leaving.

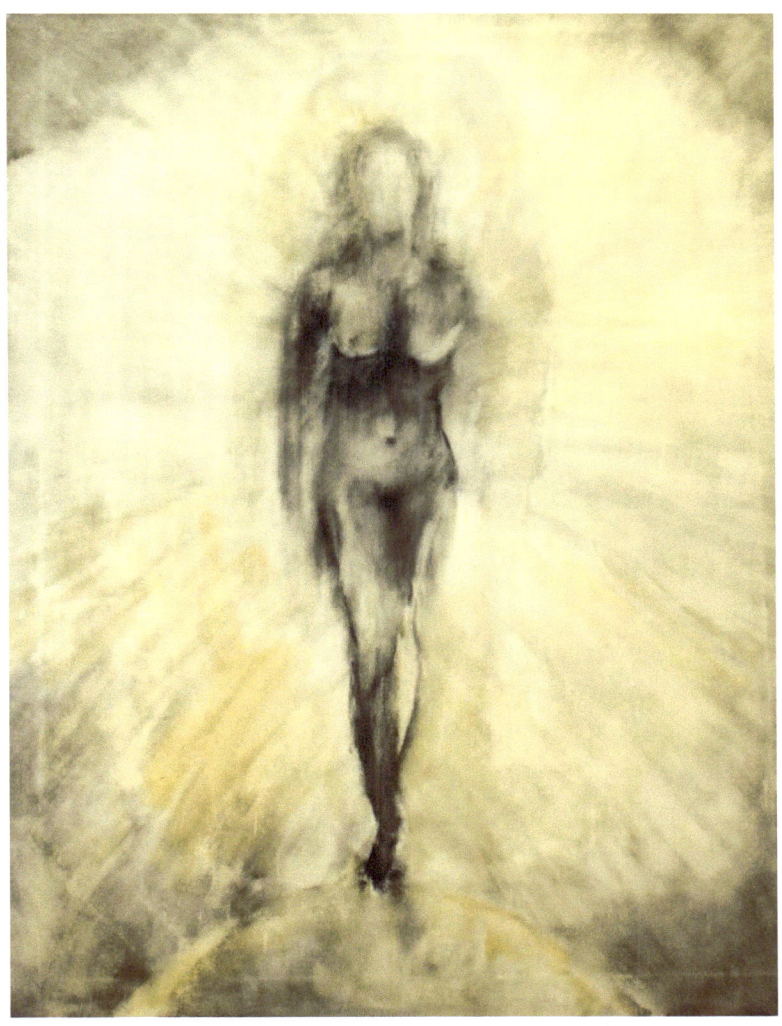

***

Everything has been left behind but the view of my body, of my presence. And my body stretches to become everything I have lost, the beauty of flowers, the fullness of grasses and leaves, the fields, the ecstatic love of another, the walking and resting, the giving of presence. It is the journey back to myself, a self that is ever more.

***

I have been so far from myself that my only choice is to seek myself through absolute self-surrender, absolute otherness. It is the self-wounding life must endure. The surrender is more than I can do. The waiting of myself is more than I can be. The darkness of my soul leaves me lost and blind. I grope along the dark walls, my hands feeling for light, for an entrance or an exit. All I can do is go on, knowing that no matter what I do or what I fail to do it will not matter. The room is enormous and whether I go on or not, the enormous darkness is mine.

***

So it is a matter of time that is no longer time, a matter of place that is no place, a matter of being that is not there. It is to be a seer and not to see. It is a way to be that is not to be. It is together forever. I go, I come, I stay, I am, I was, I shall be. Always, never, now. I am, you are, it is. Learn to count, learn to name, learn to create. And then know to be beyond being, beyond naming, beyond creation. Learn to be our name again, everything forever and ever again. It is the grace and wisdom beyond each other yet to each other. It is the continuity of again, of continuance. It is the releasing and rejoining forever and forever. It is everything to all again and constantly. It is my foot bone connected to your ankle bone, your ankle bone connected to my leg bone, my leg bone connected to your hip bone, your hip bone connected to my back bone, my back bone connected to your shoulder bone, your shoulder bone connected to my neck bone, my neck bone connected to your head bone, your head bone connected to our dream. It is one, it is two, it is the pairing, it is the separating, it is the relating. It is again, a place and time where awareness and feeling embrace and join and become again.

***

I fall yet again, my deaths without end. I no longer live my life, my wounding is beyond boundaries. Where is there the warm light on my skin? What is the image that forgives? How can I be ever again? I need your gift tonight, your light. Bathe me in your round heart. Sing me into your arms. Let my passion be received. My eyes have seen the wonder of you, let my tears wash deep your vision into my soil. Let my mind flow into your blood to reach your far heart. And if I send my words to you, will you hear me? Our voice fills the field tonight in an echoing chorus. I am yours. May my self-emptying be yours, may my call find you, may my eyes circle full and whole, may the dream awaken.

***

Enter the swirl and circle all the others. In the midst of the dance is the wild momentum of your motion, from a distance, when no longer a dancer, is the elegant pattern of the dance's turnings, the swirling mystical body of experience and thought, the rhythmic embrace of my steps and my intention. I will circle myself into you.

***

This morning the branches are filled with snow, the sun shimmering their surface. It is this luminous emptying that is the surface that reflects it all, its beautiful branches of white falling down.

***

I fill my home with flowers, with spirals within circles, shapes that empty and fill simultaneously. I embrace a shape that releases. Let soon flowers open to fullness, let eternity be seen and loved in time.

***

It is the flowers we seed, the flowers we wear. It is how we feel, where we think, what we pick to wear. It is the wearing of the world. It is the subject

and object of emanation to be immanent. It is to be
worn. In beauty it is. In the night and the day it is.
In the flowing of now into eternity it is. In the flowing
of eternity into now it is again. In the mind that is
free of thinking it is, in the flowing of eternity into
now it is again. It is to go, it is to stay. It is to go on
and it is to not. It is the proceeding that goes back, it
is the going back that proceeds. And in the thought is
the action, in the will is the heart. And it is only a
matter of time and it is time that matters. You have
such a long way to go, such a long way to stay. It is
to let and it is to go. It is the mind letting to itself, it
is the heart letting to its shape. Sleep, go on, awake,
let. It is late and it is early. It is time. It is the far
field of our lush hearts where our blood flows like
rain. It is the shape of the field we become. Sleep, go
on, be. It is to be the far field. It is the falling of
leaves over the field, it is the fall that leaves. It is
Summer into Fall and it is the fall of together again.
It is my foot bone connected to your soil, your soil
connected to my leg, my leg connected to your roots,
your roots connected to my back, my back connected
to your trunk, your trunk connected to my shoulder,
my shoulder connected to your branches, your
branches connected to my neck, my neck connected to
your leaves, your leaves connected to my head, my
head connected to your fruit. It is the field together
again. Return to the body of the field. I am you and
we are again together. We are the shape from fence
to far fence, from sunrise to sunset, from night to day.
We are the resurrection of together and again forever
again. We are the resurrection of the field made flesh,

of the flesh made again the far field. I am you and we are again. Let us again.

***

In the snow and wind, along a path bordered by you, your quiet full enough to break the heart, your world such a wondrous body, your lullaby such a long lament sung through many seasons with a harmony I can but barely grasp. And yet I now know your song can reach and join the singing of my heart in a union of sound beyond my mind, and become the shared breathing of our being.

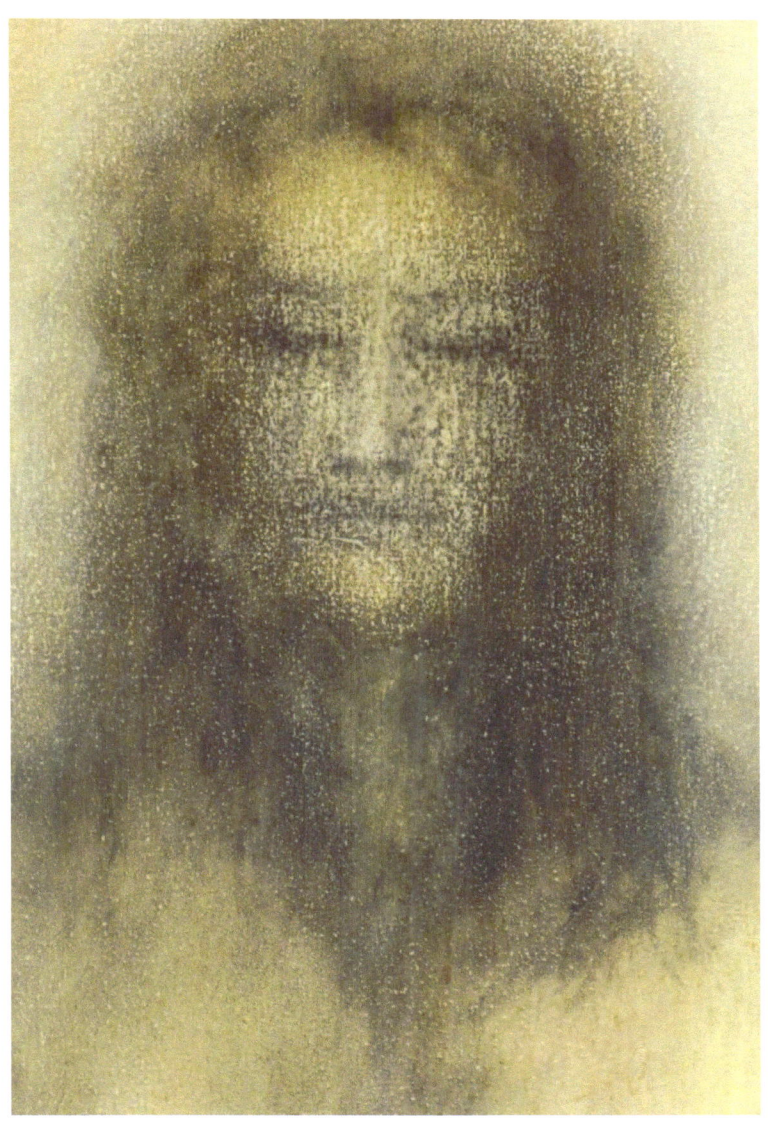

***

A beautiful morning, the sun shining onto the many leafless trees a color like burnished rust, and gold splashing onto your swirling purple dress. We enter light in the wonder and gash of our clothing draped around the field of the world. It is not us at all, but you.

***

And I will wait for you. Help me to become empty enough so you may find room to enter. You take so much room. I have had to remove everything, a lifetime of desires. When you come will you bring gifts? I have no light, will you bring illumination? I have always preferred loving in light. I have no food, will you bring nourishment? I have no clothes, will you bring bright colors to cover me? I have no memory or dreams, will you bring pictures and images to soothe with beauty? I have no words, will you bring me songs? I have no lover, will you bring me love and laughter? I have no soul, will you see me? I have no mind, will you know me? I have no body, will you hold me? I am nothing, will you be me? When there is enough room for you, there is no room. When there is enough space, then spaciousness is without room. When there is no more me, then finally there is no you. And we embrace. Help me to empty the room of myself. When I can no longer see myself, will you kiss my eyes?

***

Tonight I rid myself of the dreams both well dreamt and badly dreamt, of the memories both mine and others', of the hopes and losses spacious enough for beauty. I accept it all and I refuse it all. I welcome change and I slam shut the door. I ask and I live without requests. I am dreaming my life and my eyes are wide open. I want nothing and I want everything. I am chaos and I am unity. I am many moments allowing love and beauty, anger and shock and defeat. I surrender and I rebel. I am an angel with the odor of an unwashed body. I am a flower whose roots bring to beauty the nourishment of rot. I am the sacrifices and the saved. I am the now of an eternity of death and life. I feed on both and know not the difference. I am again and I am never. Taste lingers in my mouth like old breath. I swallow and I vomit. I grow in dying. I am sunk deep in the delight of a flower. Lost deep in the rot of my roots spills the waste of beauty. I wait the cycles and I curse time. I wither and I grow and in my growing wither again. The petals of my heart open and close in an anguish and a delight beyond my help. The gash of my color is a shimmer that wounds and heals. I dwell in a translucent darkness and in a light that darkens. In the long night of today I dream my thoughts and am dreamt by my body. Farewell everything, your emptiness feeds me. And emptiness is so enormous. Like the soft edges of water my memories and acts fold inward, old, rotting, falling. And when I open my eyes I remember old tears. I correspond. I close my eyes to these memories and the salvage of myself. By morning I promise to forget again.

***

When you meet me you may not even know me, may not even know who you have become. We stand together looking out into a large flat field. I have come to bring you away.

***

In the last light birds sing across the field into the approaching dark. Their call soothes. When will I walk again in ordinary grass? When will my voice return to greeting? I am so close to myself. It is such a beautiful time between today and tonight, between who I am and who I will be. Let me walk again the field with no place to go, let me open my language to the body of myself, to simply call to you. Dear tree of life and death open your new leaves to me, my arms will wave you. My old rebirth I am tired for you, your roots grow long searching for the nourishment of my tears. I nourish you in my dying, in my waxing and waning out of my dark. My rain bathes your wounds. My sadness is a part of my seasons, my reason for leaving you each year. We present ourselves in such greetings. Do you hear the bird's song through your hair? Answer them if you will. And I will quietly be there with you, my branches a nest for this journeying.

***

The moment of birth has left me exhausted in my search for anything so as not to undergo the total reformation of myself. Yet the words of my world can no longer nourish me. It is the child that dreams the dying. And it is birth that dreams the child. The memory is to let the dreamer and the dreaming coincide, to create and be created by the creating, like a child to dream yourself dreaming, to think yourself thinking, to be yourself being.

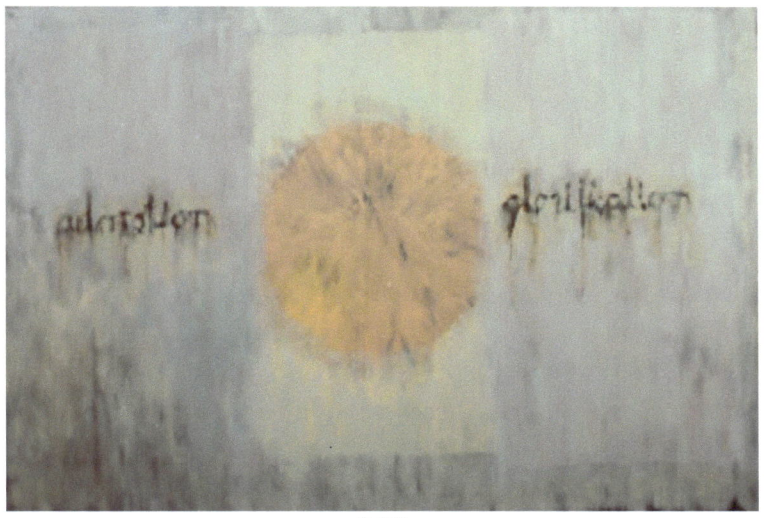

***

I listen to the birds singing to the morning light and imagine what it would sound like not to desire, to hear the rhythm of relating without the desperation of holding, where the call of relating dissolves coming and going into a fullness that is still, an interpenetration of form and formlessness where nothing and everything embrace in sameness. If I truly dreamed I would be the body of everything stretching infinite all directions, where near and far are close at hand, a circle of seeing and seen.

***

The journey into you is such a long way, an artery revering through vast grasses, gathering the body of the world to itself, remembering where it has been and where it will go.

***

It is time we go and it is time we stay. Eternity is only around the corner, only near an open heart, the sun shining into outstretched arms. It is the face in the sun. Look into the sun and see us all. We are in the field. It is north and it is south. It is east and west. Yesterday and tomorrow are today. And it is the cross that stretches to them all to become a forest. Yesterday and tomorrow are today. What we did and what we will do are the same. Our embrace is forever. All you have to do is step into eternity to reach now, to meet us, to find us here. The waiting takes no time at all. It is only around the corner, through the window, to the sun shining back our faces onto the field. I have been waiting all my life for you. And only now do I know the waiting was over all my life. There is no waiting, there is no separateness. The mirror and the reflection are the same. The dream and the dreaming contain each other. The imagination and the imagining are united. We are only the moments of our heartbeats shaping the field. We never found each other because we were never lost. Eternity and now are the same moment. To go home is to stay and to stay is to go home. There is no place to be, no time to spend. There is only our shape letting go, shining the sun back from the field to itself, where the field and the sun create each other. A gift to let now be, to let us all. The field and we are one at last. I am you and we are here at last. And the time it took us to arrive lasts because it is no longer time. Be patient and wait and know you are no longer waiting and never did. Stand together in the field, but a few feet apart, and know you are no longer standing apart but are the field. And know your being for the first time again. And know that everything is gathered again and ever again. It is everything to all always, a coherence beyond meaning that means everything. It is not why. It just is. It is a mystery where the contents are known as they change. It is the freeing gift of the field where the gift of love is the gift of loving, where the gift of presence is the gift of becoming by being.

***

A day of old habits of forgetfulness. Soon I will be old again and this will be something to leave again. Will I want to come back as I must once have wanted? Will your voice reach across to me, to reach the quiet where you are, where there is no coming, no going? It is late and it is early, the road beginning to darken, and I cannot see the distance. And I am tired, neither saddened nor hopeless, simply going home to all that is you.

***

Let your rain flow to slowly sway by body into you. And I will shimmer and wave like silken petals reflecting and absorbing all that is. And the field where I am will be gladdened. I will give myself away to birds on their flight into beauty. My yellow sleeves will nest all into the body of my branches. And my fragrance will be an odor radiating infinitely in all directions, at last open enough to accept everything. I stand swaying in the night among the fireflies, their million eyes flashing into my face.

***

The field is my shepherd, I shall not want. It maketh me to lie down in pastures of green. It leadeth me beside the waters of stillness. It restoreth my flesh. It leadeth me in the paths of creation for its name's sake. Yea, though I walk through the valley of the darkness of night, I will fear no longer, for it art with me. Its grasses and its trees they comfort me. It prepareth a place before me. It anointest my head with rain, my flesh runneth over. Surely growth and beauty shall follow me all the seasons of my life. And I will dwell in the place of the sun forever.

***

Early morning, a soft rain, the crying of birds, my mind and heart exhausted, the early light forsaken through clouds, all falling down like tears of myself. I sleep into the image of a castle where a woman is preparing a banquet, the interior illuminated by golden light, the entrance a pair of enormous doors slowly opening, the carillon of music gently and quietly inviting me inside. Can you hear this wonder? Come into my heart, its doors open wide. I am in the country of you. Still your weeping, your loneliness is not what you know it to be. When will you truly love me?

***

I destroy all structures, all definitions. I fling from me the mind, the body, the soul, myself and what is not mine. I will possess none of it. Nothing nor no one shall embrace my scattering. If you call me I will not hear you. My ears roar the buzzing of chaos. If you see me I will not look at you. My eyes are burnt black in vision. I stand in a garden and the fire of my breath burns it all. I am in the ashes. And I am burning golden flowers to illuminate myself. Find the charred ashes of my love. Take these offerings in your hands and release them across the field. Fling me as far as the wind can scatter. I would be regathered in a new season, swaying in young grasses. You may never find me again, for in my flinging I will be with my lover at last. After all the burning I will be free.

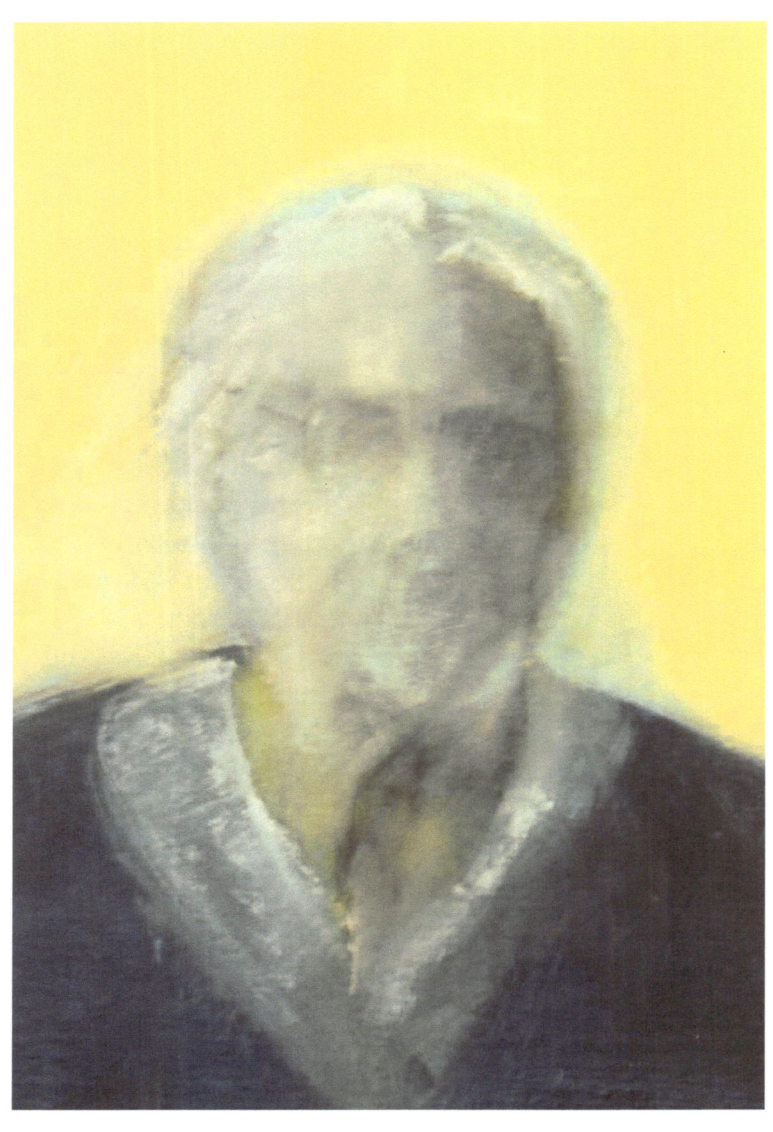

***

     O foolish one, your declension roots so deep in search of light. Open your eyes in ascension to the color of yourself. In the moon's light listen to the geese on the distant pond. Let your light stream upward to answer their cries. Stop your foolishness and abide for awhile. Soon the flight of your wings will shower light in dazzling directions, splashing color back onto the pond.

***

To give and to receive without loss or gain, to endure the reality of what we are is the way from inwardness to openness to otherness. To explore the limits of perception and feeling is to go beyond everything back to everything. And at the boundaries of the mind to find not ourselves but another. When you can no longer know then and only then can you be revealed. When you can no longer be, then you can become what you are. When you have no place else to go, then and only then can you be where you have always been. Now that I am with you, let me put aside myself and sit with you. After all these years I am so close to you. Your hiding all these years was perfect, by being so close you remained far away.

***

And it is every second and it is every minute and it is every hour and every day and every month and every year and every now and every eternity. And it is everything of the field. I am, you are, it is, we are, thou art, they are. Let us all. Let and go and be and look to the field and see us all. And the field and the sun will see you. Then walk through the field, through yourself, to where I am. And we will see each other. Would you meet me in the country of our bodies? Let the rain flow down your face and into your soil to nurture and swell and shape the forming field of our bodies. Walk the paths and arteries into yourself. You will reach where I am, standing in the green and red of the field with my yellow on. And will we dance and play in the field of our hearts. And again will finally be to gain, to gain our body and blood, to gain the shape of our creation. My foot bones connected to my ankle, my ankles connected to your leg, your legs connected to the field, the field is connected to us all. Let us again. We are in the field. Could you find me there? Could you find thee?

***

My eyes close and I descend, falling, crashing through and splintering a network of connecting supports. I watch as second by second, minute by minute I fall at a swift even freedom into infinity. I look down to see if there is any bottom. Nothing but a fall into forever. I reach out and stop myself. A rope immediately appears and I let go of my hold and reach out to it. Slowly I am pulled upward. When I finally reach the surface there is no one nor nothing but an empty expanse. All is bathed in muted light. Steps appear descending down either side of a pyramid. I step down one side and sit on the pyramid's base, a child waiting in the sun on the stone steps of my childhood home.

And a child standing in the lawn, its eyes shimmering greeting to wonder, before its long voyage into the effort of time and destiny. It takes my breath away and becomes the only answer to why. I am so old and so new. I am a child of God's long duration, creation's endless restoration. I am the beginning and the ending each and every moment. I am what there is after time and self, a child sitting in quiet light on the stone steps of approaching memory. The long life waiting for me is simply all I have forgotten. I knew of it from the beginning, it was there in my eyes all along. Somehow I knew all along I would find and meet you, would love you. The dreams I have always known I will always be. I have already been where I will go. I am my great return, my turning back to you, my love refound. I form myself in everything. I am at last unseparate.

***

Can we love enough to be identical, with each other, with everything, with all, with each and every view, smell, sound, to mean as it all means, to be all always and forever, to be the oneness within that is without, to know time and space beyond now, beyond any and every moment to the stillness, emptiness, and fullness of being, where now is freely given back, to go beyond the very possibility of being able to live, able to die, to the timeless time-bound reality of intention? To find meaning in everything and then to let go of the meaning of everything, to embrace the mystery of being and then to let go into becoming, to think with the shape of the heart and then to die its rushing pulse into the space of the body of everything. To go beyond creator and creation to their love. Go beyond it all to the stillness of all sensation, all unity. You can never love enough unless you are able finally to awaken to a new dream, a better dream, a dream that is ultimately what dreaming can be and should be, the creativity of loving enough. It is the psalm and palm at the end of the heart. You can never love enough unless you can die enough, can endure the mystery and pain of your deaths and births. If you can somehow find the grace to die enough you can love enough. I dream of myself and of another. I dream of the reconciliation beyond structures, the marriage and joining of everything to all, always and forever. I dream the final dream of time flowing into the still pond of now, the I at the center of sight, the now that is no longer now, the past, the present, the future of eternity, the ecstatic presence, the space of the being of creation, the grace of presentation, the face at the end of the mind, the opening and closing of the eye, the I at the beginning of the mind, the heart that is mine, the answer when the questions cease, the sound after all the calling, the unknown that knows, the ineffable that is touched and released by the palm of being, the child in the lap, the tree in the field, the field in the sun, the sun slanting back into the field of your child's lap.

***

You have two choices dear self, either know who you are or surrender to who you are. Neither way is easy. There are no hierarchies in this. The only talent is patience. The only reward is loss, spacious and unending. And I am so lost. I am no longer trying to reach anything for there is nothing and no place. Images and dreams collapse over me. I make them, watch them, grab them tight, and then let them all go their way into my emptiness. Let me die my deaths. Let me be common. I have reached the end of myself and I cannot see or feel or hear or taste or smell. In myself I am without reality and without illusion.

***

From the clouds of my overspreading mystery falls a day-long rain of tears, soaking and forgetful. My memory is healing, my forgiveness washing into soil. I reach back into the world to touch what I can no longer feel. It is all so far away. And it is all so near. All at once I am free. If I want all I have to do is dream, and to dream all I have to do is be. In the miracle of duration I am. I am a dream that is visible in so many ways. Let me be forever in your flowing dress of time. Let me swirl and circle my sleeves of gold to gather all into my releasing capture and dance. Your eternity is not what I thought. Your swirling dress gently held in my flowing sleeves dances the distance around us, round and around again and again. You are my return, my restoration, my dance.

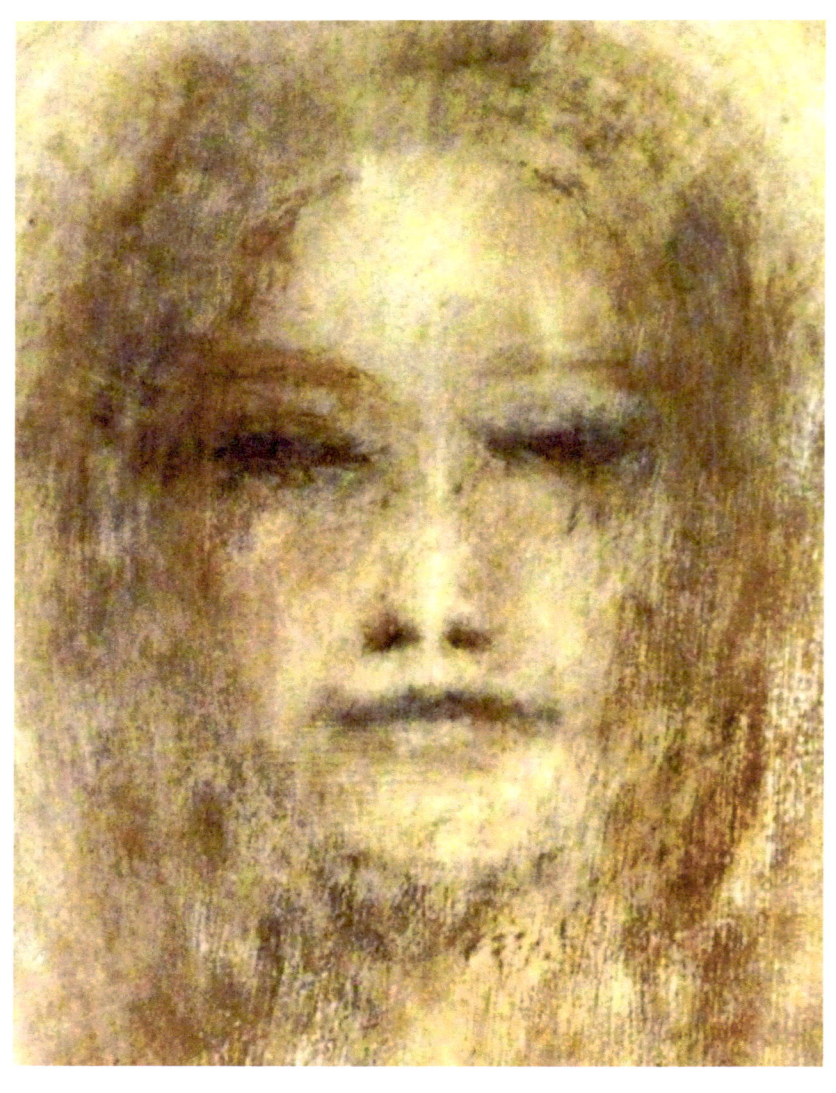

***

Our union is in our bodies, our lover, the other, joined in identity, reunited into our wholeness. We need go nowhere, to no other, the act of separation and restoration is ourselves. We are neither I nor you, but in the swirling rush of our bodies are both always. I do not embrace you any longer. I no longer search for you. I am free of my parting and love you beyond my dying. I am you in my body. We see and meet each other in ourselves. The light tonight is lasting, filled with clouds of color, flashing darkness and shimmer. I lie quietly within inches of the upper branches of the trees. My face turned into rusted leaves.

***

Begin anywhere and then let go and watch the beginning rush to where it can only go. Can we love enough, can we die enough, can we be enough? All that matters is our relationship to it all, to the dream that dreams. Let go and be given the space of it all, the act of it all. My dream of creation dreams me. I reach for an image and the image reaches for me. I search for content and the content finds my search. And our embrace is a vibration that gathers all direction, all time, all of our myriad pulses. Back and forth. In and out. Now and then and will be. I sit in light and look through glass into the night. By morning my face will disappear into it all. Can we love enough to stay until the next dark? Can we know and feel enough to be it all, through the day, through the night? Through the leaving and into the coming. Hold tight. Let go. Look about you, then close your eyes and look. Dream, think, feel, love. Then let go of all and fall into it all. Can we love enough? Only if we love enough to let it all be. It is eternity without time. And it is unconditional when loved. And my heart is so ravaged in its wisdom, so lost in its love, the shape of all I embrace. And when did I start, where is my beginning, how do I end? It is the risk of grace, the birth of eternity every second, every heartbeat, every death, every kiss, every thought, every love. Can we love enough? You have so far to go, so much to dream, so long to be.

***

You have to be willing to die to find what doesn't die. You have to be willing to fall into darkness to see. You have to be willing to lose your body to feel. And you have to be willing to lose love to give it all back. Come home again, to the body of birth, to the attention of it all, to the wings of your arms, the gently swaying branches of your legs, the nest of your heart. If you let go, you will be and will go home. It was, it is, it shall be are identical. I am, you are, we will be are the same. It is every second of every minute of every hour of every day of every year of every thought of every dream of east and west and north and south of every summer and fall and winter and spring of every now of every yesterday of every today of every tomorrow. And I am lost in it all and I am found in it all. I am nowhere and I am everywhere. Can you find me? Can you meet me? Can we love enough? It is only morning and it is already night. It is time to fall into sleep and it is time to awaken. It is the time it takes to be, to meet, to love.

***

I weep for the mind, I weep for the body, I weep for loneliness, I weep for union, I weep for love, I weep for the loss of love, I weep for flowers and beauty, I weep for hope, I weep for birth, I weep for answers, I weep for findings, I weep for dreams, I weep for rest that cannot soothe, I weep for prayers and I weep for pleasures, I weep for giving, I weep for time and for the end of time, I weep for place, I weep for eternity, I weep for waiting, I weep for courage, I weep for hunger and I weep for fullness, I weep for the past, I weep for the future and I weep the present, I weep for all that is and all that is not, I weep for sound and I weep for silence, I weep in light and I weep in darkness, I weep for coherence and I weep for chaos, and finally I weep for you, my beloved. I weep for your beauty, I weep with your pain.

***

Together is to gather. And I will go out into the world, and I will find and walk all the streets and fields of myself. I will be a farmer in the heart of the field. And when I am finished I will hold the field in my palm and know that the field and my open hand are one, a oneness where you and I sway in the gentle wind of my breathing.

***

I no longer want to be nor to become nor to have been. All sound, all sight, all smell, all taste shocks me. My body is startled by all sensation. I need my eternity. The weeping of my sleep seeps into my waking. It is in the uttering that there is pain. It is the separating out that rends the heart and body, and distances the beloved from beauty. To love and be loved is the terror thou must endure. In our fullness there is neither lover nor beloved, nothing to love, no one to be loved.

***

Lie quietly and stretch into the soil, your roots and thoughts and dreams sinking into the surrounding, your face and limbs covered by snow, listening to the voices of children sledding down your body. It is the country of your body they will play. And if you can wait, when the sun returns your hair will grow into waves of grass, your dreams will grow a world to live. Your heart will be your beauty of new leaves. All will be returned. And you will know for the first time and the last time that there was no return, there were no seasons, you were only asleep, only resting into your heart. And what is perishable is yourself, the child's voice creating forever. You were only listening all along. Awake to the country of your heart, the voice of the child playing over your body and calling its name again. Become your rebirth each day, each season, each lifetime, the wonder of your heart into infinity. Pass the time in

presence, sway your voice, your limbs, your grasses.
Breathe the breath of your voice flowing into your
heart, shaping the womb of your face. Winter but a
way to sleep away the separateness. Spring, your
morning. Summer, your life, in fall, your falling
asleep. Become the cycles of your deepest dreams,
your sleep without cycles and seasons, unfolding all
life, letting time its life to dream. If you can only wait,
there will come a time when it no longer is to dream,
when sleeping and waking will be united, when the
living of your heart will gather it all, the ice and the
snow, the rain and the sun, the day and the night.
And you will be a child's voice reunited to your heart,
falling into the folds of its skin, into what is
imperishable, the world of the body. Can we love
enough to create time, to live eternally? You will
never know unless you risk it. Give up your wide
leaves, let fall your tall grasses, let your rain weep
into your dream, let your many streams flow. Give up
your soil. Dare to find out. Go beyond your life
enough to find out if you can live. Go to sleep and
see if you can awaken. Be awake and see if you can
sleep. Go into your mind and see if you can dream.
Grow and see if you can remain, die and see if you
can go on, love finally and see if you can do
otherwise. Can you love enough to know and see and
feel and be and be loved? There are so many forests,
so many sloping fields, so many days and nights, so
many thoughts and dreams and acts, so many lives, so
many illusions, so much flesh. Dare to be it all, all
the time and all the space. It is all united beyond
itself. Rest quietly and reach into it all, into the
presence of everything. Beyond everything is again,

the voices of your children dreaming your name.
Beyond everything is the fullness of nothing, the
generations of your heart, the dream that is the heart.
Find all the images beyond the imaging, and there
you will find us. And you will have found the
emptiness of us all and the unity of us all. Let the
wind breath us all together. It is merely all the time it
takes, the blowing of our name across the field. It is
the bliss of our calling. Can we love enough is the
answer to all we can do. Let go of being and you will
be. And you will finally know how to be the child of
your body. You will be the time it takes. I cannot tell
you what it is, and yet if you were to look closely into
my eyes, I would have to tell you. I would if you love
enough want to tell you. Beyond being is where you
must live, in the flesh and in the voice beyond it all.
Leave your home and yourself, and go home even if it
takes forever. Leave and go and stay into the
presence of everything. It is the journey home to the
dreaming of that home. It is the bliss of our naming
the body of our dream. We think only in so far as we
are thought. We dream only in so far as we are
dreamt. We live only as long as we die. We go only
as far as we are led. We surrender only as much as
we are taken. And we love only in so far as we are
loved. We cannot more. We are only in so far as we
have been and shall be. I am is I was and I shall be.
And it is everything again. And being everything we
are no more. No thinking, only thought. No
dreaming only dreamt. No loving only loved. We are
a thought beyond our minds, a dream beyond our
dreaming, a love beyond our loving, a union beyond
ourselves, presence beyond our shape. And there is

nothing beyond. There is no now, no was, no shall be.
Live presence that is no longer there. Live love that
is no longer loved. Can we ever love enough is the
patience of desiring to be. And patience is beyond
our waiting. You have got to simply let go of
yourselves, of everything, to reach your being in the
far field.

***

I continue to fall through the acts and
possessions of my long life. I cannot now stop this
fall into myself. I am reeling far away in my nearness.
I have been wounded to the very beginning of my
pain. I am made near my eternity in the wonder of
time. And I search for limits. I will never find them
by remembering. Dear life, accept my body. Dear
eternity, accept my moments. Dear light, accept my
dark. May my dark prepare greater radiance. May
my pain prepare deeper union. I fall to the center,
and in my wanderings to there create the pattern of
myself. When I look back I see a flower, overlapping
petals of golden shimmer. I stand with my skin
blowing outward from the wind of my breath. My
entrapment has all along been my true shape. I billow
in the wind. Here I am. Is it I? The only way to me
is through creating, through the circling dance of
what I am. I am form and what is without form. I am
thought and its passions. I am the body and its
dreams. I make form and form remakes me. I am the
dance of being in and out of itself. The voice of
many lives asks always the same thing. Where are
you? My questions are so many echoes, so many

answers, so many memories, so many loves. The grasses, the leaves, the flowers, the mind and its memories sways in wind and rain over the far field.

**

And finally past it all I dream again. I dream that you will be there in the field. Who are you? Will you be there to meet me again? Be this dream and know that you are being dreamt. Let us soon meet in a field of quiet beauty, in the presence of all we are all the time, creation and created, a last field of embrace. Who am I? I am you. Who are you? You are. Through Union, to Hope, to Liberty, to you. It is the journey round place and time, from there to here, the journey to you. And now at last I find myself so many times and ways. Past us all is the infinite touch and look of us all. And our face is all there is, shimmering in the eyes of everything. And in the attention of everything we are finally identical, a unity of time and space in change that cannot change. The gift of our sacred heart is the fullness and emptiness of its blood, the pulse of everything forever, the reunion of our union, the dying that gives birth, the now of always, the knowledge and love beyond life and death, the quiet of the dreamless dream and the stillness of forever, the ecstatic space of all communion, the field of our being. Take this lawn, this meadow, this field, its grasses and trees, its flowers, its sky and wind, its color and darkness, seasons and passages, for this is your body and blood, which is given to you in your name. Take it and be of

*it always. Beyond it all to the far field of vision
where God is everywhere and I live myself.*

***

*Dear self, become at last your soaring to it all,
always and again. You are awaiting yourself, the
nest of your startled body. Become the space of your
flight into the startle. Fly to it all in the far field of
yourself where your lover awaits you. Through
Union to Liberty, welcome home Holy Spirit to the
open palm holding the field. It is all alright, for you
could not have known it was impossible to hurry.*

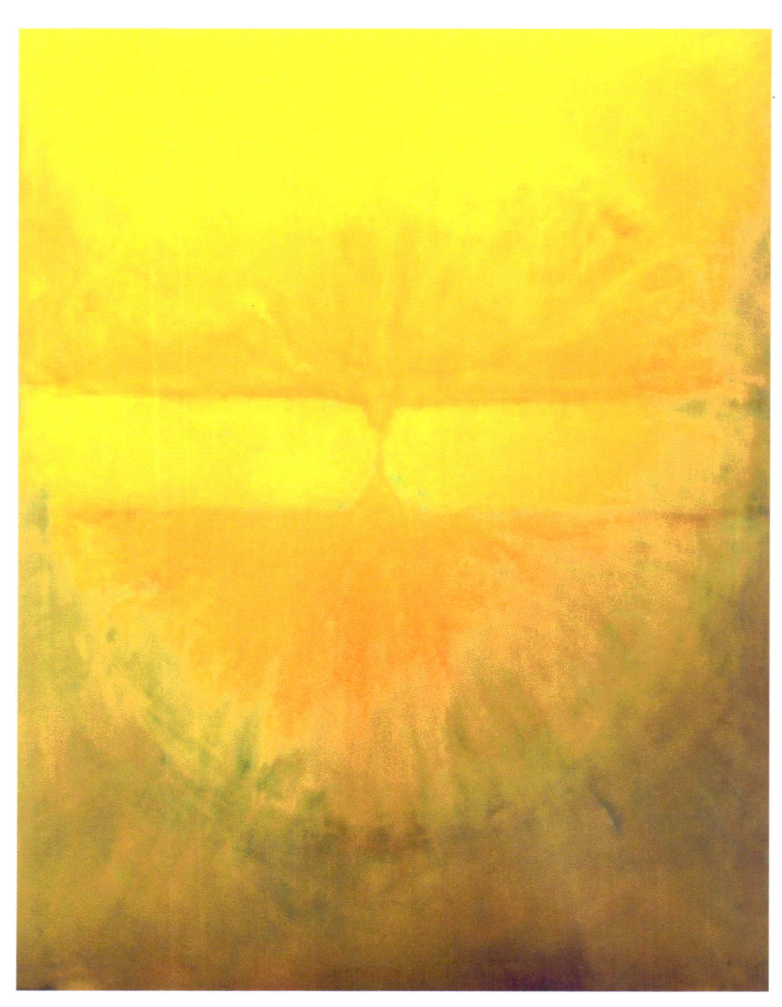

www.ingramcontent.com/pod-product-compliance
Lightning Source LLC
Chambersburg PA
CBHW040844180526
45159CB00001B/314